Learning With Money Activity Kit

by David E. McAdams

Once they realize what money can do, children love money! Their attraction to money helps them learn to count, add, multiply, and handle large numbers. Inside, find ideas for using play money to aid learning. This book contains $2,805,768 in play money to cut out and use to learn math. There are 24 of the $100,000 bills, 24 of the $10,000 bills, 24 of the $5,000 bills, 24 of the $500 bills, 48 of the $100 bills, 48 of the $50 bills, 72 of the $20 bills, 48 of the $10 bills, 96 of the $5 bills, 24 of the $2 bills, and 120 of the $1 bills.

David E. McAdams has written many math books for children, plus several books on other subjects. His hobbies include writing books (of course), programming computers, gardening, and designing websites. He thoroughly enjoys his children and grandchildren.

Copyright 2020 Life is a Story Problem LLC. All rights reserved.

Other Books by David E. McAdams

Parrot Colors – An introduction to the concept of colors. For preschoolers.

Flower Colors – An introduction to the concept of colors. For preschoolers.

Space Colors – An introduction to the concept of colors. For preschoolers.

If I had a Monster – A day in the life of a four-year-old with monsters as daily companions. Coming soon. For preschoolers.

Shapes – An introduction to shapes. For preschoolers.

Numbers – An introduction to the concept of numbers. For grades K-2.

What is Bigger Than Anything? (Infinity) – An introduction to the concept of infinity. For grades 1-3.

Where does the Water Go? – An introduction to waste water treatment for grades 1-4. Coming soon.

Swing sets (Sets) – An introduction to set theory. For grades 2-4.

One Penny, Two – If Sig's penny doubles each day, how long until he can buy a dark green sports car? For grades 3-6.

Learning With Money Activity Kit – Teach large numbers and counting with over $1,000,000 in play money.

My Favorite Fractals – A picture book of wondrous fractals presented as high resolution images. For all ages.

The First Million Digits of Pi – The first million digits of pi. For all ages.

e to One Million Digits – The first million digits of the Euler's constant e. For all ages.

The Square Root of 2 to One Million Digits – The first million digits of the square root of 2. For all ages.

Orders of Ten – A book that illustrates orders of ten with dots (1, 10, 100, … dots). For ages 10-15.

Geometric Nets Project Book – 80 geometric nets to copy, cut out, and tape together into 3 dimensional polyhedra. For ages 9 and up.

Geometric Nets Mega Project Book – 253 geometric nets to copy, cut out, and tape together into 3 dimensional polyhedra. For ages 9 and up

For an up to date list, go to www.DEMcAdams.com.

Learning activities with play money

1. **Value, reading numbers**. Show the student a bill. Ask, "What is the value of this bill?"
2. **How much**. Put a few bills in a pile. Ask, "How much money is in the pile?" Or, put some bills in a wallet and ask, "How much money is in the wallet?"
3. **Equality**. Show the students a larger bill and smaller bills. Ask, "How many of the smaller bills do you need to be the same value as the larger bill?"
4. **Multiplication**. A toy costs $2. You want to buy one for yourself, one for your brother, and one for a friend. How much do you need?
5. **Fewest bills**. A new drone costs $123. What bills can you use to pay for it? Which bills would you use to pay with the fewest bills.
6. **Total**. Gather some groceries and put a sticker on each with a price. Ask, "What is the total?" Have the student show which bills they would use to pay the total.
7. **Rounding up**. Tell the student an amount. Ask, "How many $10 bills do you need to pay for this?"
8. **Have enough**. Give the student some bills. Ask, "Do you have enough to buy a pony for $100? How much more do you need?
9. **Race to $20**. Give each of a group of students some bills between $1 and $10. Each student places one of their bills in a pile by turn. If a student puts a bill on the pile that makes the value of the pile $20, they win. If a student puts a bill on the pile that makes the value of the pile over $20, they are eliminated and the game starts over.
10. **More**. Show two bills to the student. Ask, "Which is worth more?" Sometimes, show two bills of the same denomination.
11. **Money war**. Mix up a bunch of bills. Deal the bills to the students playing the game. At each turn, each student pulls one bill off of the top of their stack and place it in the middle. If one student places a bill larger than any of the others, that student wins. If more than one student has the largest bill, they pull four bills off of the top of their stack. The game continues with the fourth bill being the one that may decide a round.
12. **Find the denominations.** Give a riddle such as: Jill's total is $16. She pays with four bills. What combination of bills did she pay with?

Learning With Money Activity Kit by David E. McAdams

Learning With Money Activity Kit by David E. McAdams

Learning With Money Activity Kit by David E. McAdams

100,000
THE
UNITED STATES OF AMERICA
100,000
ONE HUNDRED THOUSAND
DOLLARS

100,000
THE
UNITED STATES OF AMERICA
100,000
ONE HUNDRED THOUSAND
DOLLARS
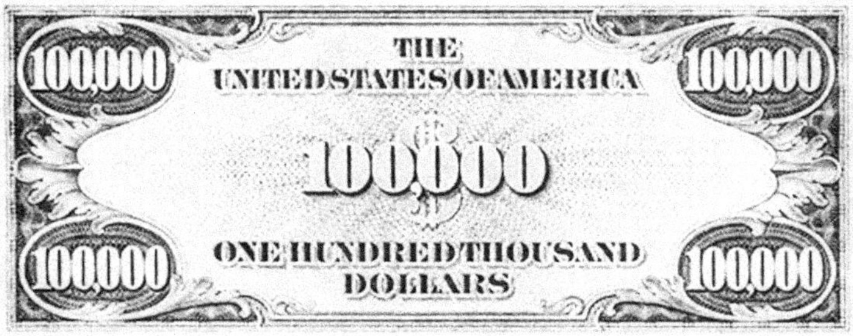
100,000
THE
UNITED STATES OF AMERICA
100,000
ONE HUNDRED THOUSAND
DOLLARS

100,000
THE
UNITED STATES OF AMERICA
100,000
ONE HUNDRED THOUSAND
DOLLARS
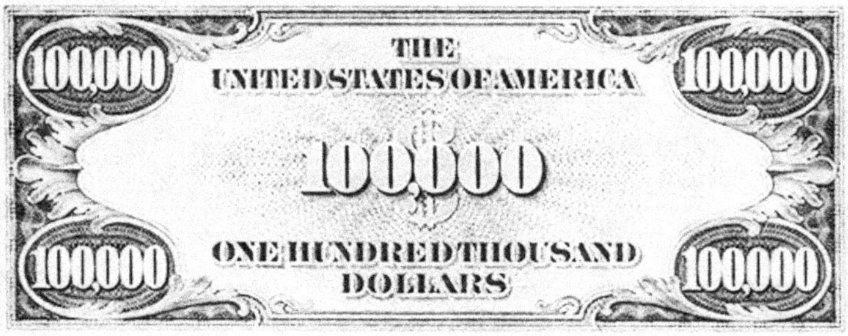
100,000
THE
UNITED STATES OF AMERICA
100,000
ONE HUNDRED THOUSAND
DOLLARS
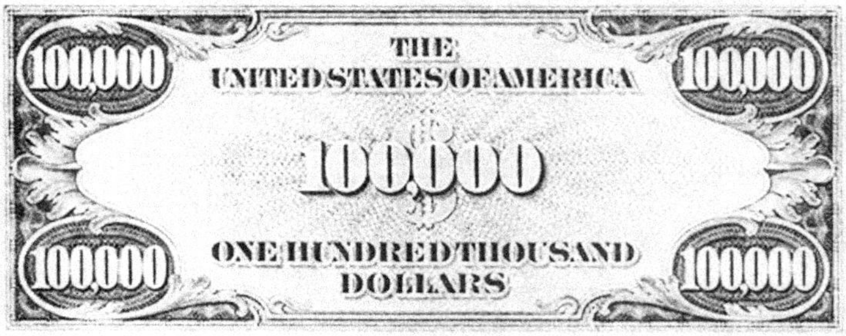
100,000
THE
UNITED STATES OF AMERICA
100,000
ONE HUNDRED THOUSAND
DOLLARS

100,000
THE
UNITED STATES OF AMERICA
100,000
ONE HUNDRED THOUSAND
DOLLARS

100,000
THE
UNITED STATES OF AMERICA
100,000
ONE HUNDRED THOUSAND
DOLLARS
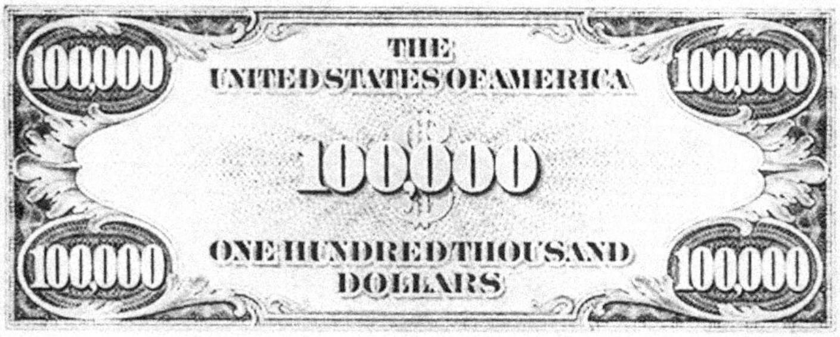
100,000
THE
UNITED STATES OF AMERICA
100,000
ONE HUNDRED THOUSAND
DOLLARS
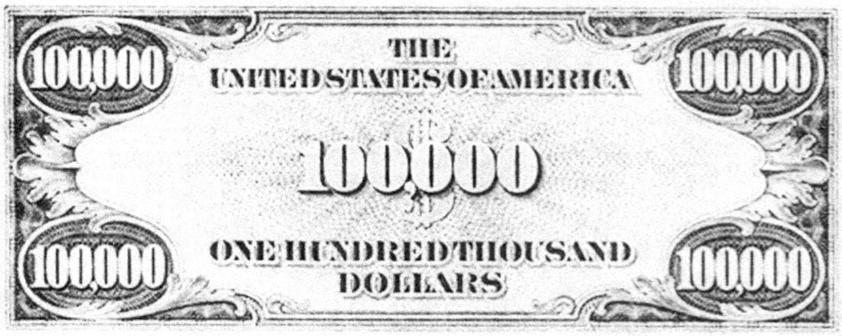
100,000
THE
UNITED STATES OF AMERICA
100,000
ONE HUNDRED THOUSAND
DOLLARS
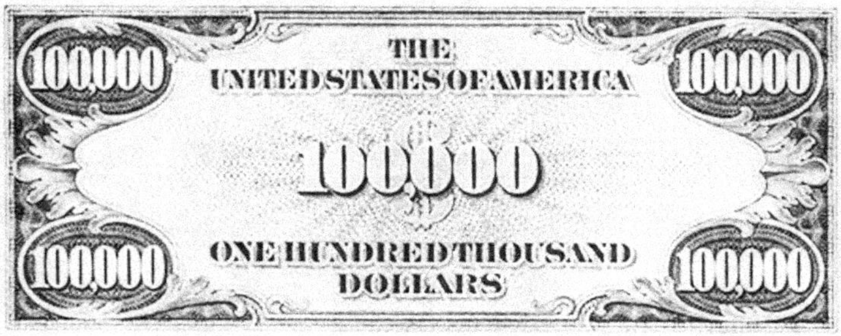
100,000
THE
UNITED STATES OF AMERICA
100,000
ONE HUNDRED THOUSAND
DOLLARS

100,000
THE
UNITED STATES OF AMERICA
100,000
ONE HUNDRED THOUSAND
DOLLARS

Learning With Money Activity Kit by David E. McAdams

Learning With Money Activity Kit by David E. McAdams

Learning With Money Activity Kit by David E. McAdams

Learning With Money Activity Kit by David E. McAdams

5000
THE UNITED STATES OF AMERICA
GOLD CERTIFICATE
THIS CERTIFICATE IS A LEGAL TENDER IN THE AMOUNT THEREOF IN PAYMENT OF ALL DEBTS AND DUES PUBLIC AND PRIVATE
A00000001A
Play Money
MADISON
WASHINGTON, D.C.
SERIES OF 1928
FIVE THOUSAND DOLLARS
IN GOLD COIN PAYABLE TO THE BEARER ON DEMAND

5000
THE UNITED STATES OF AMERICA
Play Money
FIVE THOUSAND DOLLARS

5000
THE UNITED STATES OF AMERICA
Play Money
FIVE THOUSAND DOLLARS

5000
THE UNITED STATES OF AMERICA
Play Money
FIVE THOUSAND DOLLARS

5000
THE UNITED STATES OF AMERICA
Play Money
FIVE THOUSAND DOLLARS

5000
THE UNITED STATES OF AMERICA
Play Money
FIVE THOUSAND DOLLARS

5000
THE UNITED STATES OF AMERICA
Play Money
FIVE THOUSAND DOLLARS

5000
THE UNITED STATES OF AMERICA
Play Money
FIVE THOUSAND DOLLARS

5000
THE UNITED STATES OF AMERICA
Play Money
FIVE THOUSAND DOLLARS

5000
THE UNITED STATES OF AMERICA
Play Money
FIVE THOUSAND DOLLARS

5000
THE UNITED STATES OF AMERICA
Play Money
FIVE THOUSAND DOLLARS

5000
THE UNITED STATES OF AMERICA
Play Money
FIVE THOUSAND DOLLARS

LEARNING With Money Activity Kit by David E. McAdams

Learning With Money Activity Kit by David E. McAdams

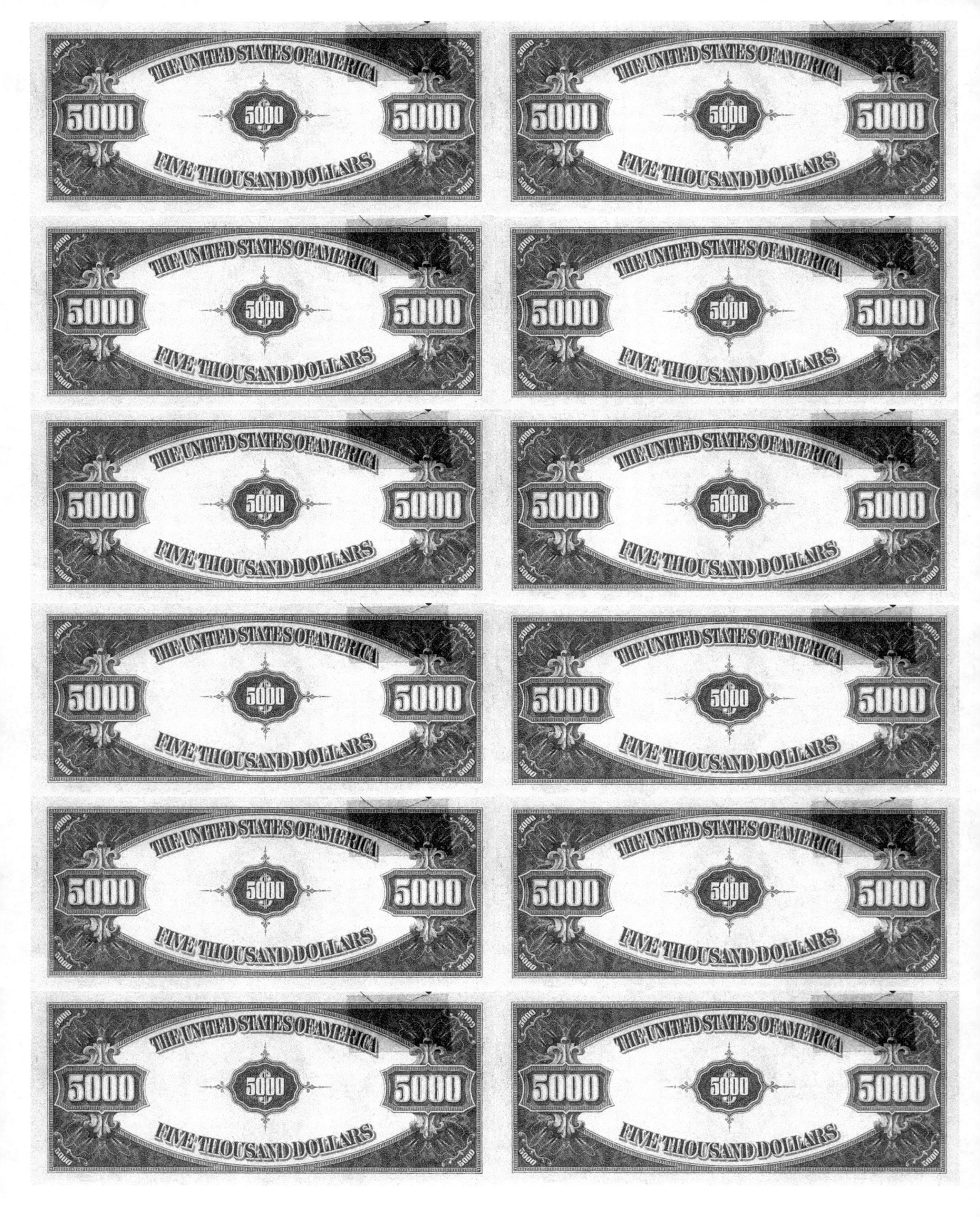

14 Learning With Money Activity Kit by David E. McAdams

Learning With Money Activity Kit by David E. McAdams

Learning With Money Activity Kit by David E. McAdams

Learning With Money Activity Kit by David E. McAdams

18 Learning With Money Activity Kit by David E. McAdams

Learning With Money Activity Kit by David E. McAdams

Learning With Money Activity Kit by David E. McAdams

Learning With Money Activity Kit by David E. McAdams

500
THE UNITED STATES OF AMERICA
500
FIVE HUNDRED DOLLARS
500

500
THE UNITED STATES OF AMERICA
500
FIVE HUNDRED DOLLARS
500

500
THE UNITED STATES OF AMERICA
500
FIVE HUNDRED DOLLARS
500

500
THE UNITED STATES OF AMERICA
500
FIVE HUNDRED DOLLARS
500

500
THE UNITED STATES OF AMERICA
500
FIVE HUNDRED DOLLARS
500

500
THE UNITED STATES OF AMERICA
500
FIVE HUNDRED DOLLARS
500

500
THE UNITED STATES OF AMERICA
500
FIVE HUNDRED DOLLARS
500

500
THE UNITED STATES OF AMERICA
500
FIVE HUNDRED DOLLARS
500

500
THE UNITED STATES OF AMERICA
500
FIVE HUNDRED DOLLARS
500

500
THE UNITED STATES OF AMERICA
500
FIVE HUNDRED DOLLARS
500

500
THE UNITED STATES OF AMERICA
500
FIVE HUNDRED DOLLARS
500

500
THE UNITED STATES OF AMERICA
500
FIVE HUNDRED DOLLARS
500

Learning With Money Activity Kit by David E. McAdams

24 Learning With Money Activity Kit by David E. McAdams

Learning With Money Activity Kit by David E. McAdams

26   Learning With Money Activity Kit by David E. McAdams

Learning With Money Activity Kit by David E. McAdams

Learning With Money Activity Kit by David E. McAdams

Learning With Money Activity Kit by David E. McAdams

Learning With Money Activity Kit by David E. McAdams

Learning With Money Activity Kit by David E. McAdams

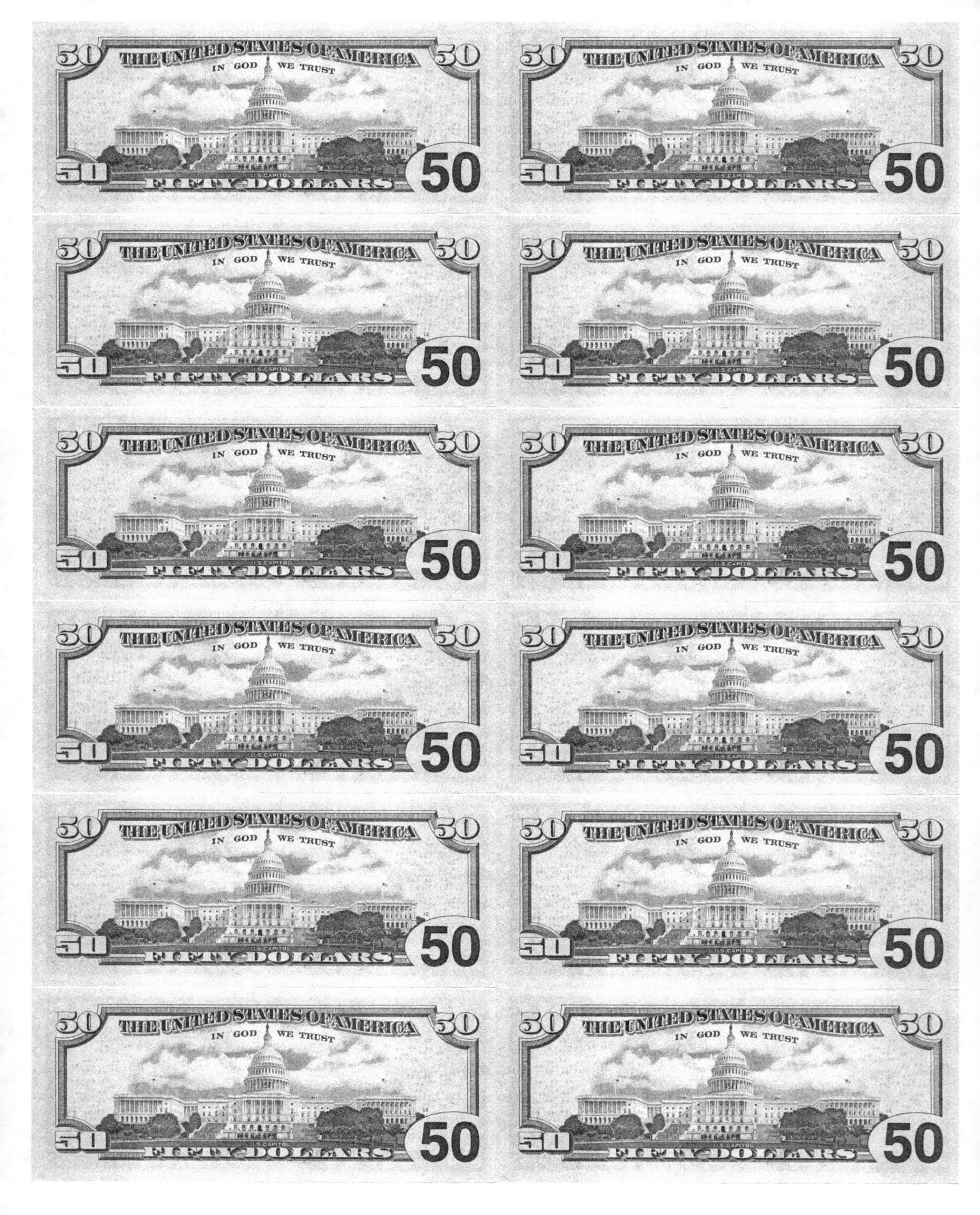

Learning With Money Activity Kit by David E. McAdams

Learning With Money Activity Kit by David E. McAdams

THE UNITED STATES OF AMERICA
IN GOD WE TRUST
50
FIFTY DOLLARS

THE UNITED STATES OF AMERICA
IN GOD WE TRUST
50
FIFTY DOLLARS

THE UNITED STATES OF AMERICA
IN GOD WE TRUST
50
FIFTY DOLLARS

THE UNITED STATES OF AMERICA
IN GOD WE TRUST
50
FIFTY DOLLARS

THE UNITED STATES OF AMERICA
IN GOD WE TRUST
50
FIFTY DOLLARS

THE UNITED STATES OF AMERICA
IN GOD WE TRUST
50
FIFTY DOLLARS

THE UNITED STATES OF AMERICA
IN GOD WE TRUST
50
FIFTY DOLLARS

THE UNITED STATES OF AMERICA
IN GOD WE TRUST
50
FIFTY DOLLARS

THE UNITED STATES OF AMERICA
IN GOD WE TRUST
50
FIFTY DOLLARS

THE UNITED STATES OF AMERICA
IN GOD WE TRUST
50
FIFTY DOLLARS

THE UNITED STATES OF AMERICA
IN GOD WE TRUST
50
FIFTY DOLLARS

THE UNITED STATES OF AMERICA
IN GOD WE TRUST
50
FIFTY DOLLARS

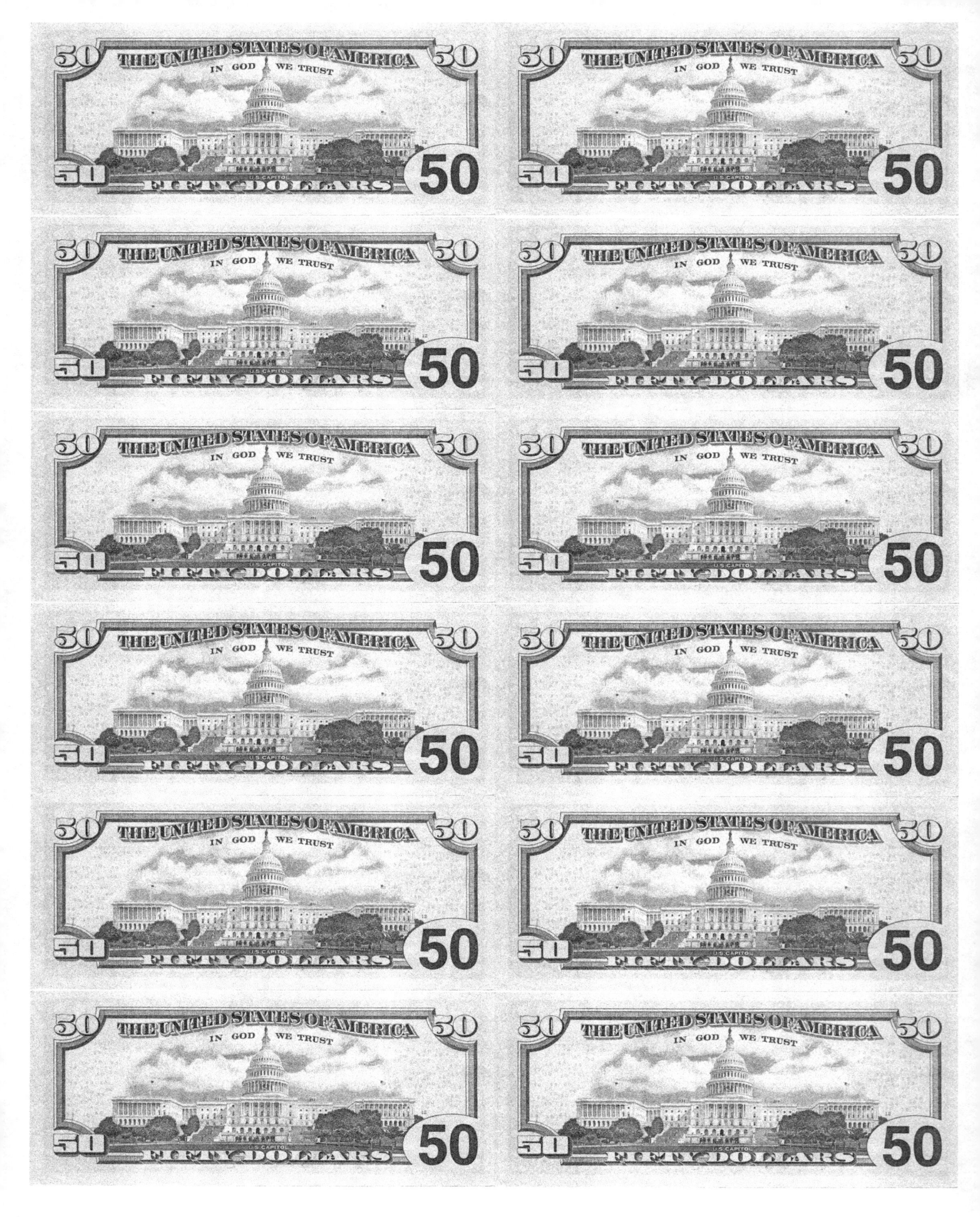

Learning With Money Activity Kit by David E. McAdams

Learning With Money Activity Kit by David E. McAdams

Learning With Money Activity Kit by David E. McAdams

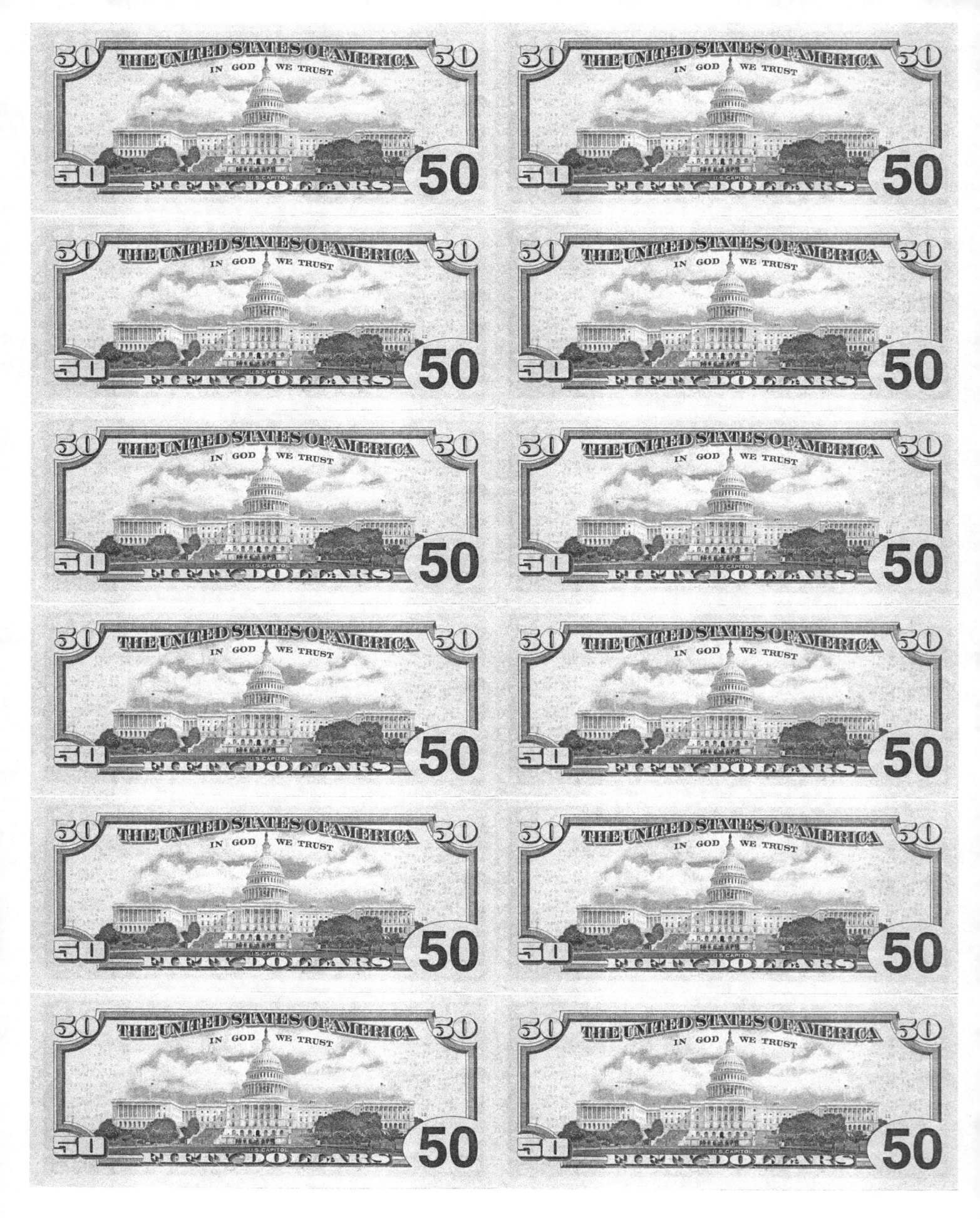

Learning With Money Activity Kit by David E. McAdams

Learning With Money Activity Kit by David E. McAdams

Learning With Money Activity Kit by David E. McAdams

Learning With Money Activity Kit by David E. McAdams

Learning With Money Activity Kit by David E. McAdams

Learning With Money Activity Kit by David E. McAdams

Learning With Money Activity Kit by David E. McAdams

Learning With Money Activity Kit by David E. McAdams

Learning With Money Activity Kit by David E. McAdams

Learning With Money Activity Kit by David E. McAdams

47

Learning With Money Activity Kit by David E. McAdams

Learning With Money Activity Kit by David E. McAdams

Learning With Money Activity Kit by David E. McAdams

Learning With Money Activity Kit by David E. McAdams

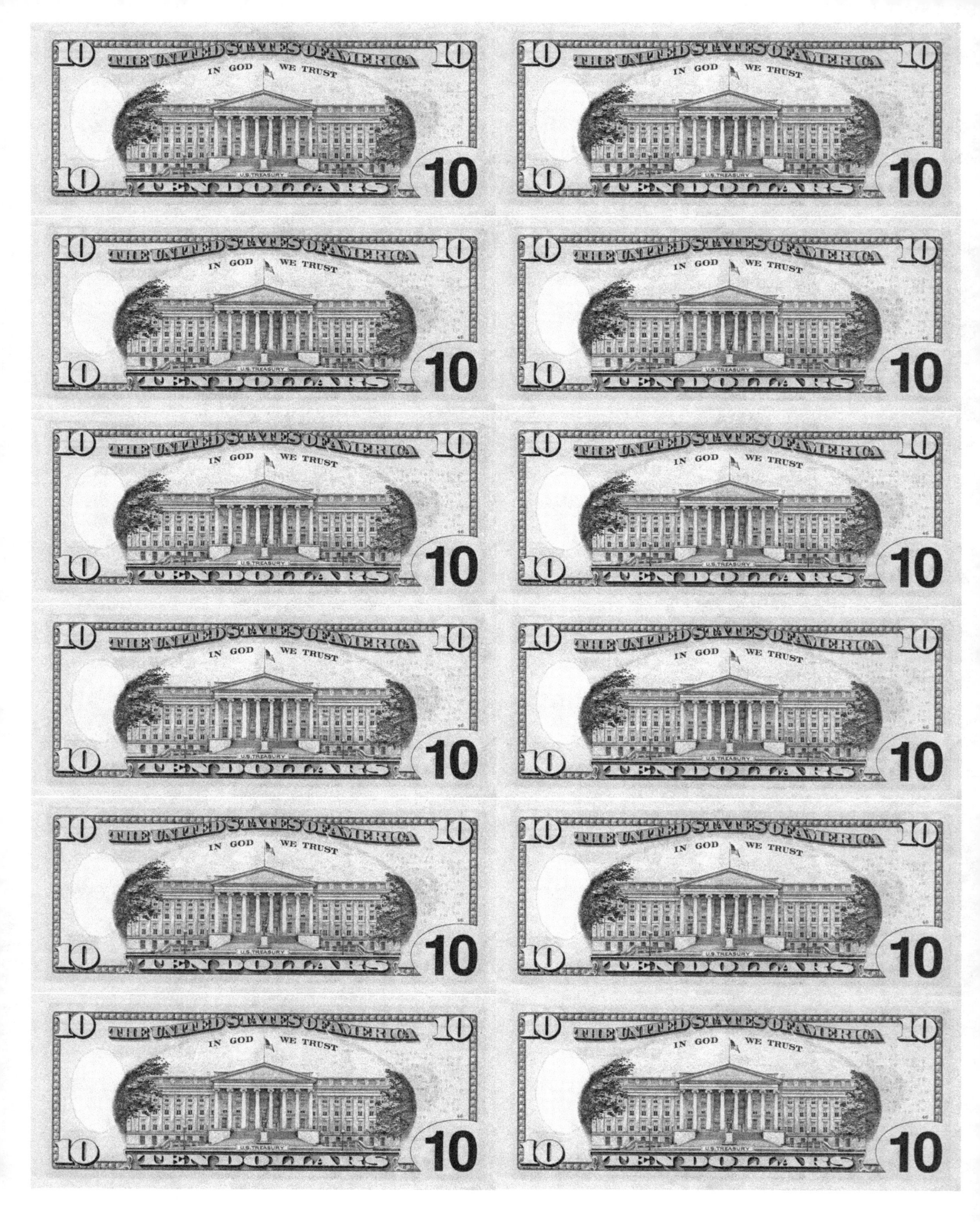

Learning With Money Activity Kit by David E. McAdams

Learning With Money Activity Kit by David E. McAdams

10
THE UNITED STATES OF AMERICA
IN GOD WE TRUST
TEN DOLLARS
10

10
THE UNITED STATES OF AMERICA
IN GOD WE TRUST
TEN DOLLARS
10

10
THE UNITED STATES OF AMERICA
IN GOD WE TRUST
TEN DOLLARS
10

10
THE UNITED STATES OF AMERICA
IN GOD WE TRUST
TEN DOLLARS
10

10
THE UNITED STATES OF AMERICA
IN GOD WE TRUST
TEN DOLLARS
10

10
THE UNITED STATES OF AMERICA
IN GOD WE TRUST
TEN DOLLARS
10

10
THE UNITED STATES OF AMERICA
IN GOD WE TRUST
TEN DOLLARS
10

10
THE UNITED STATES OF AMERICA
IN GOD WE TRUST
TEN DOLLARS
10

10
THE UNITED STATES OF AMERICA
IN GOD WE TRUST
TEN DOLLARS
10

10
THE UNITED STATES OF AMERICA
IN GOD WE TRUST
TEN DOLLARS
10

10
THE UNITED STATES OF AMERICA
IN GOD WE TRUST
TEN DOLLARS
10

10
THE UNITED STATES OF AMERICA
IN GOD WE TRUST
TEN DOLLARS
10

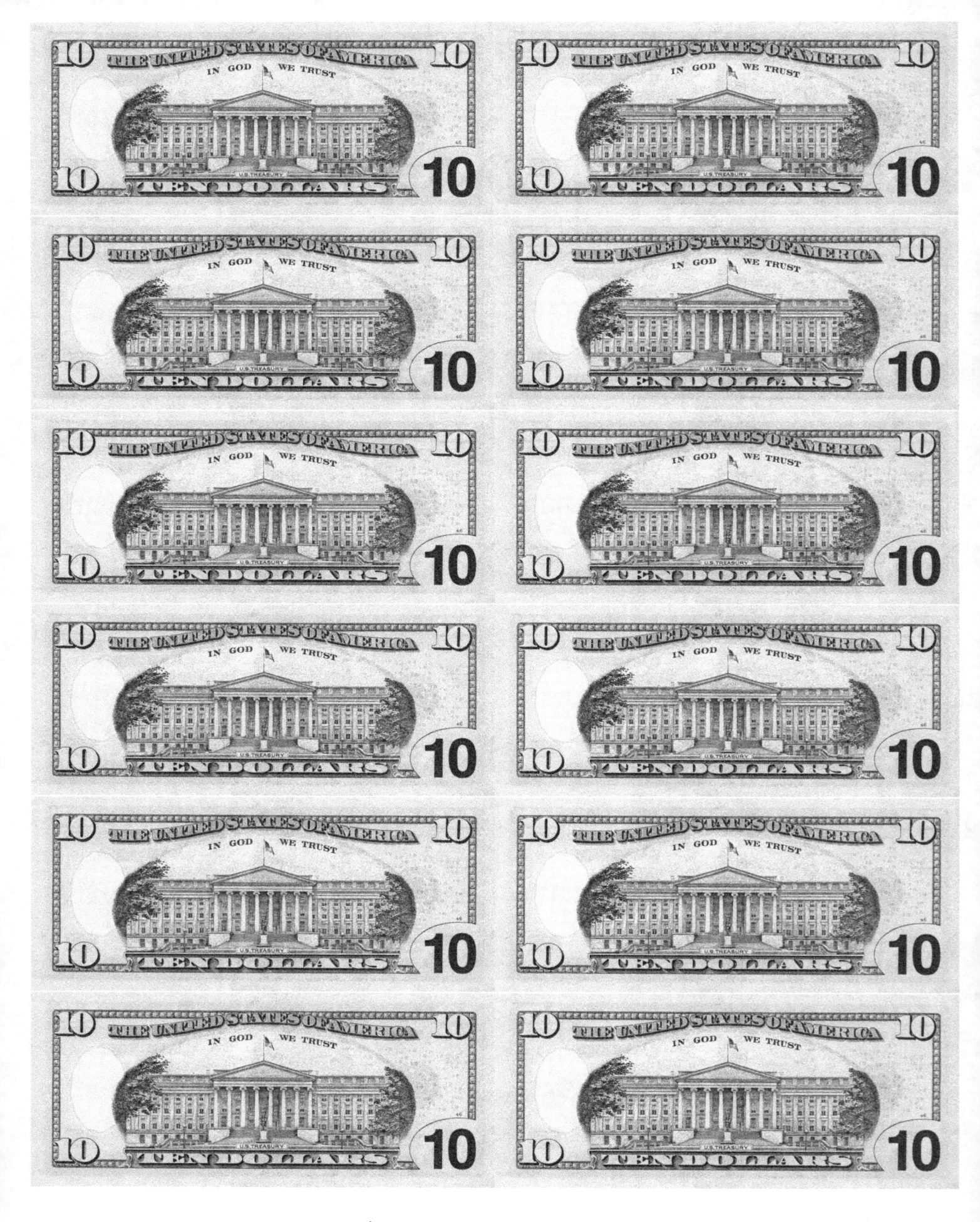

Learning With Money Activity Kit by David E. McAdams

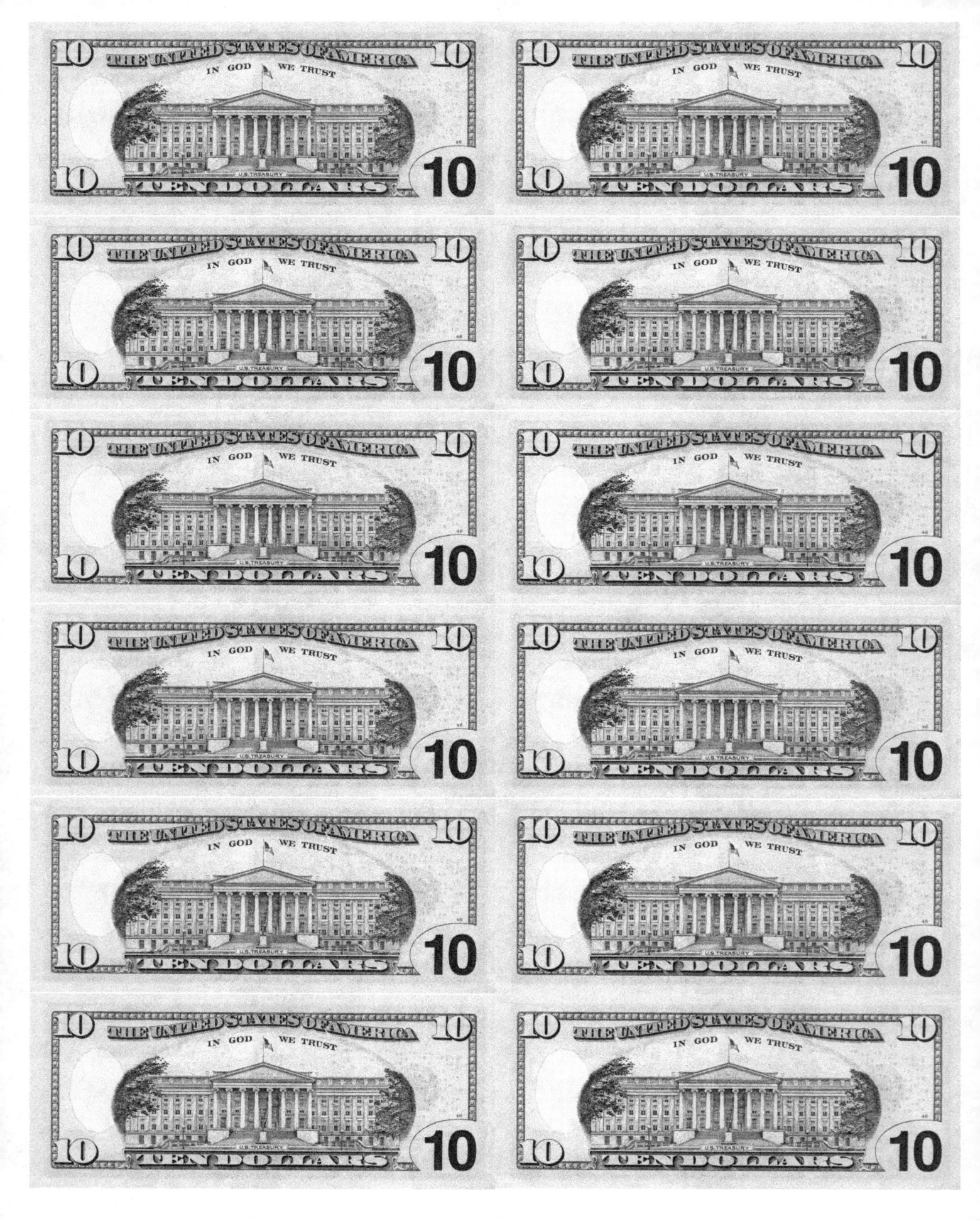

Learning With Money Activity Kit by David E. McAdams

Learning With Money Activity Kit by David E. McAdams

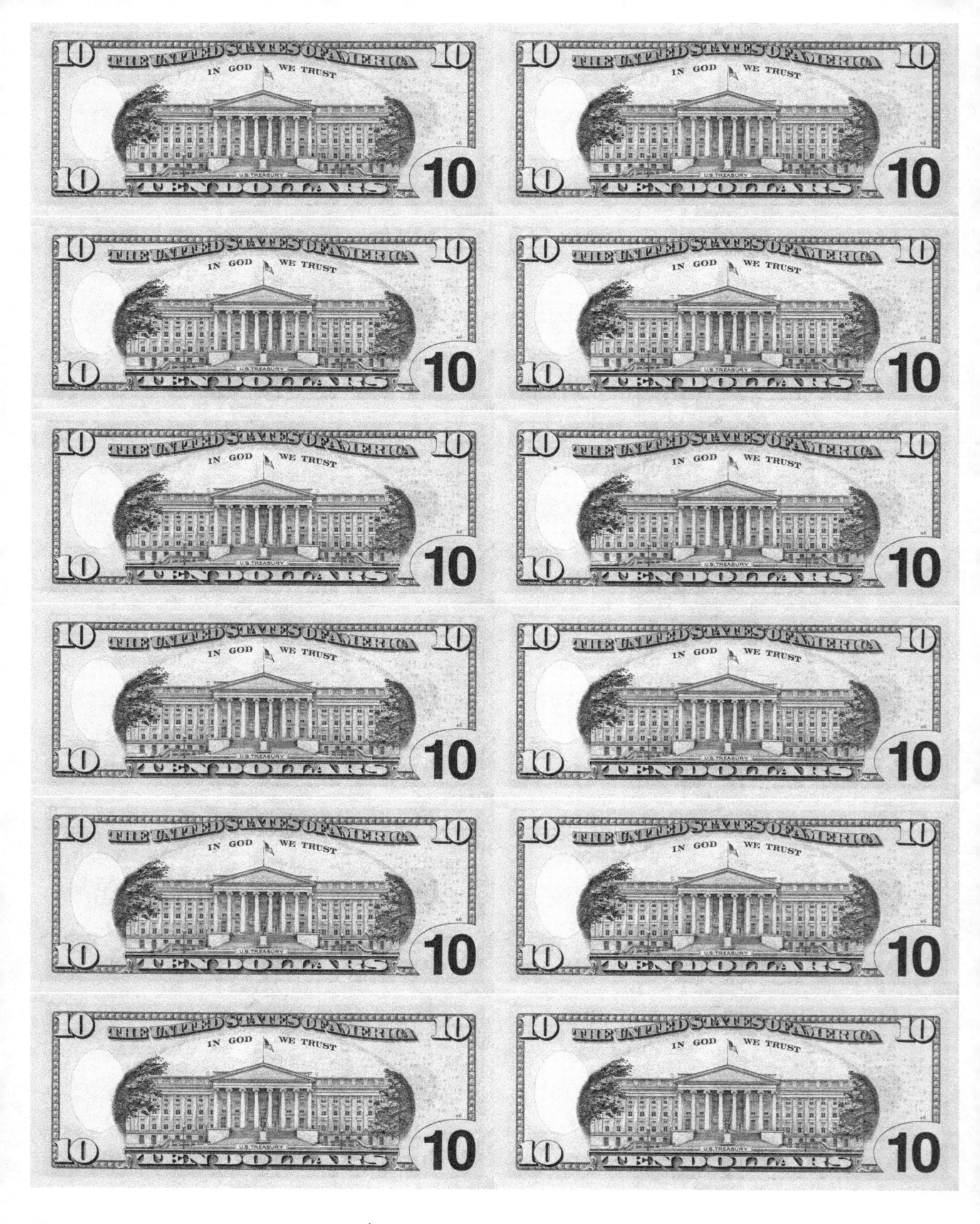

58   Learning With Money Activity Kit by David E. McAdams

Learning With Money Activity Kit by David E. McAdams

THE UNITED STATES OF AMERICA
IN GOD WE TRUST
FIVE DOLLARS
5

THE UNITED STATES OF AMERICA
IN GOD WE TRUST
FIVE DOLLARS
5

THE UNITED STATES OF AMERICA
IN GOD WE TRUST
FIVE DOLLARS
5

THE UNITED STATES OF AMERICA
IN GOD WE TRUST
FIVE DOLLARS
5

THE UNITED STATES OF AMERICA
IN GOD WE TRUST
FIVE DOLLARS
5

THE UNITED STATES OF AMERICA
IN GOD WE TRUST
FIVE DOLLARS
5

THE UNITED STATES OF AMERICA
IN GOD WE TRUST
FIVE DOLLARS
5

THE UNITED STATES OF AMERICA
IN GOD WE TRUST
FIVE DOLLARS
5

THE UNITED STATES OF AMERICA
IN GOD WE TRUST
FIVE DOLLARS
5

THE UNITED STATES OF AMERICA
IN GOD WE TRUST
FIVE DOLLARS
5
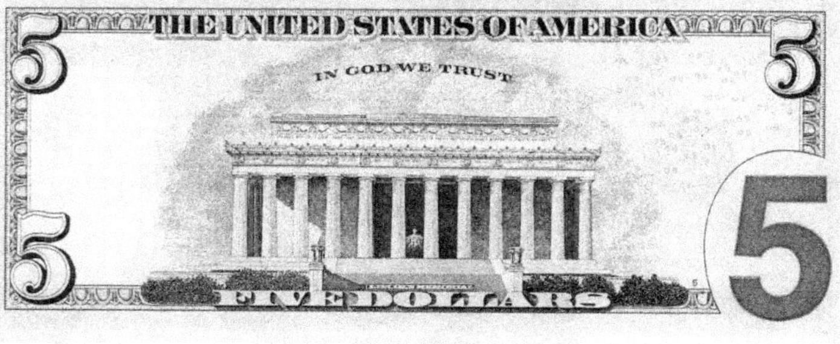
THE UNITED STATES OF AMERICA
IN GOD WE TRUST
FIVE DOLLARS
5

THE UNITED STATES OF AMERICA
IN GOD WE TRUST
FIVE DOLLARS
5

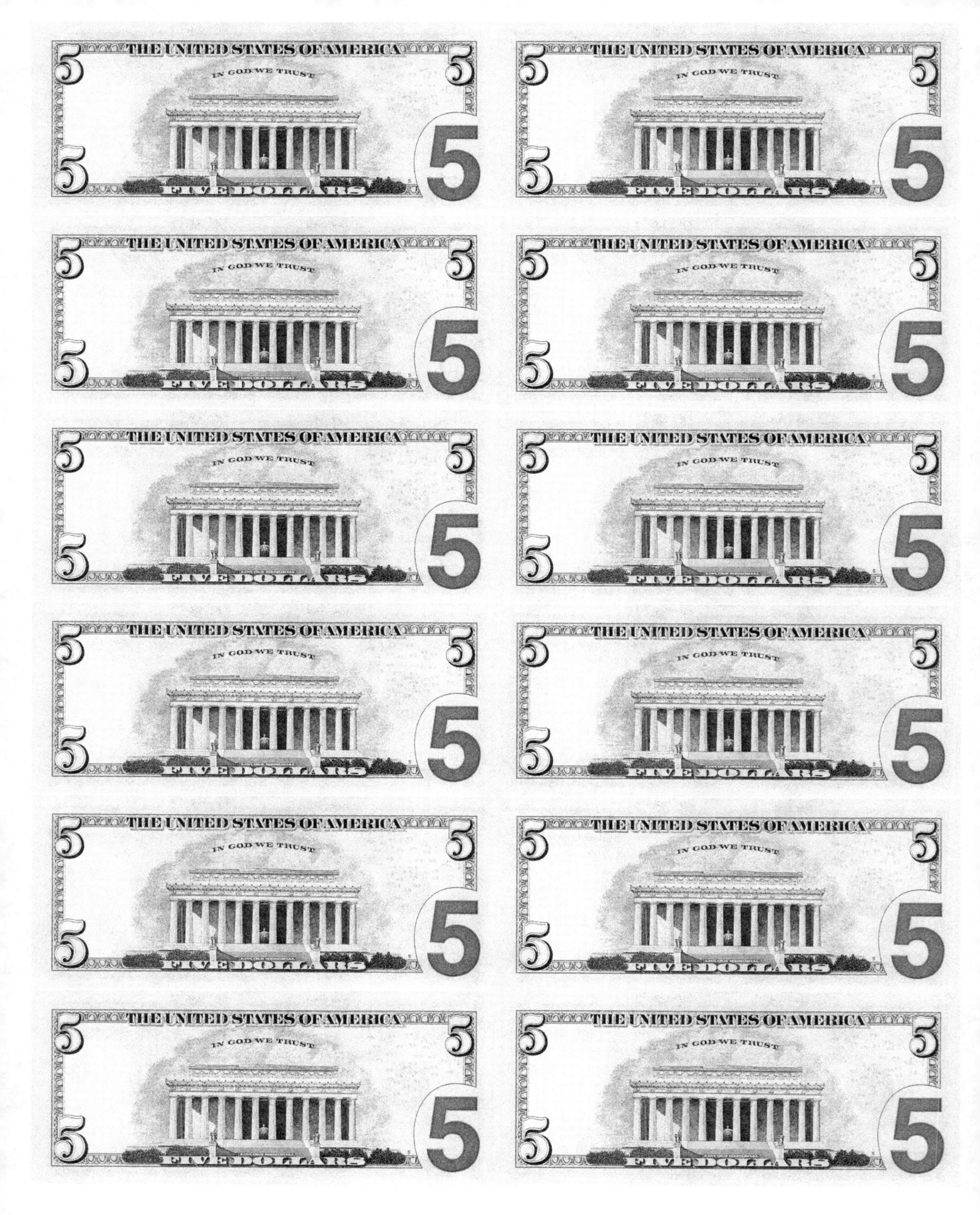

Learning With Money Activity Kit by David E. McAdams

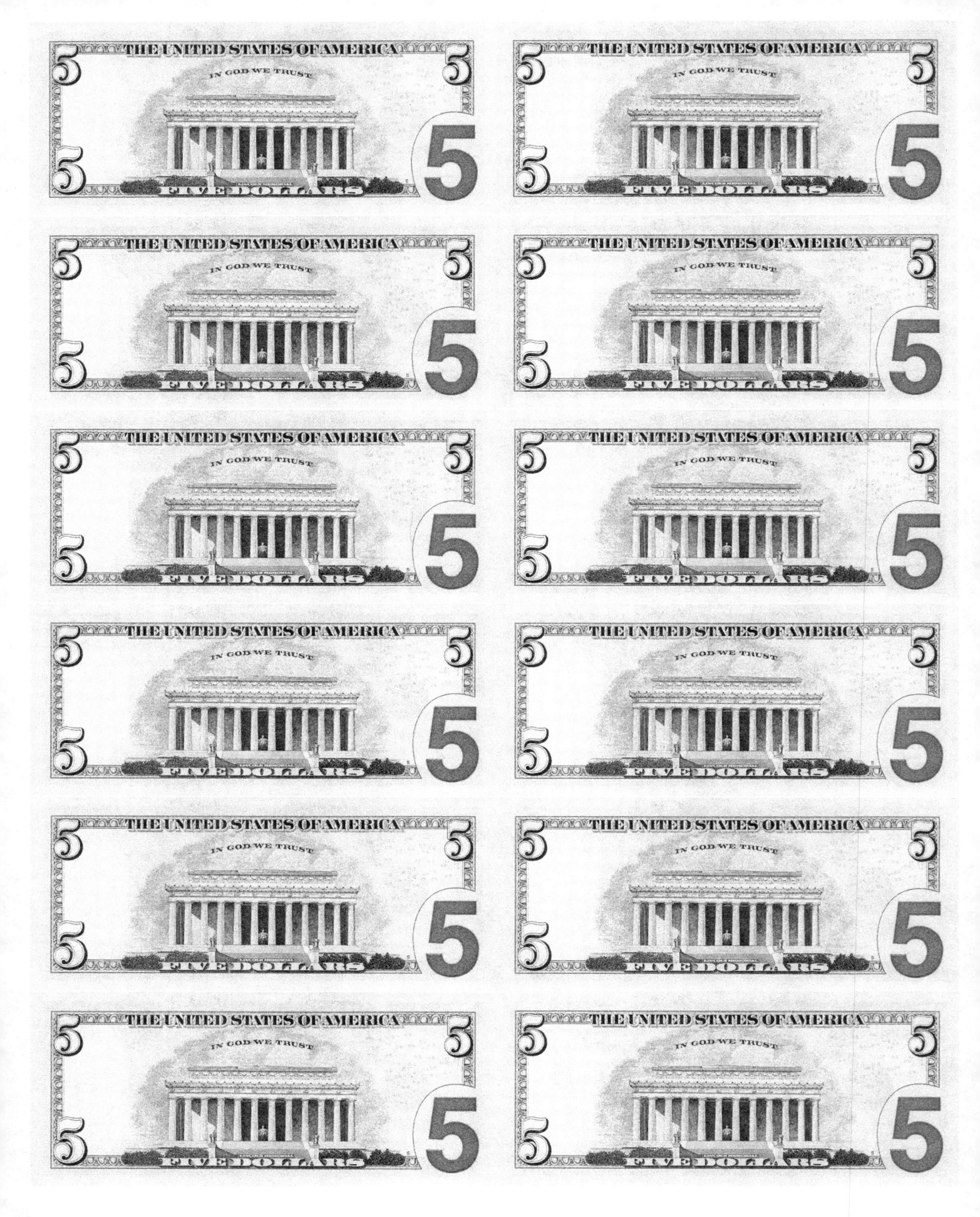

Learning With Money Activity Kit by David E. McAdams

Learning With Money Activity Kit by David E. McAdams

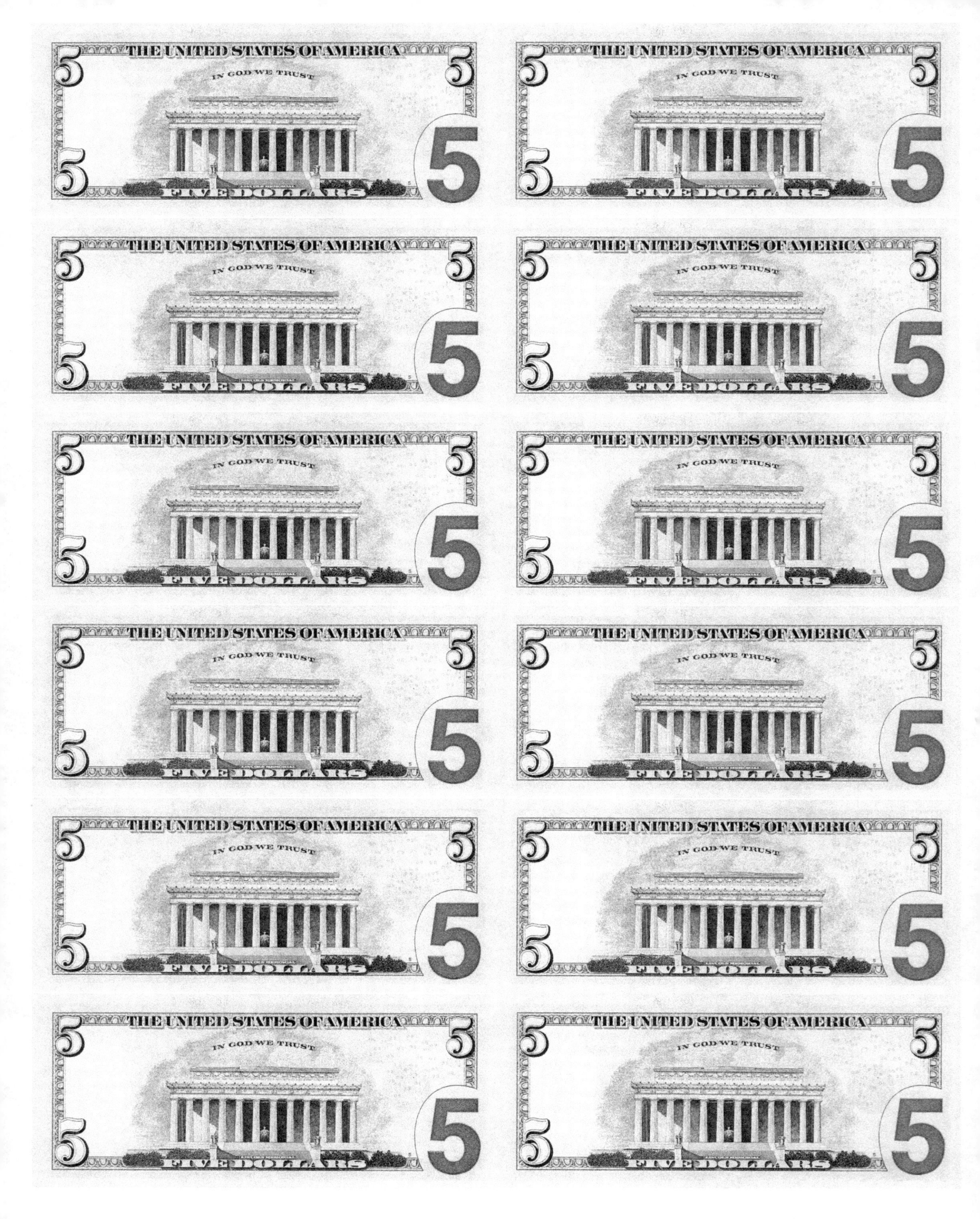

64   Learning With Money Activity Kit by David E. McAdams

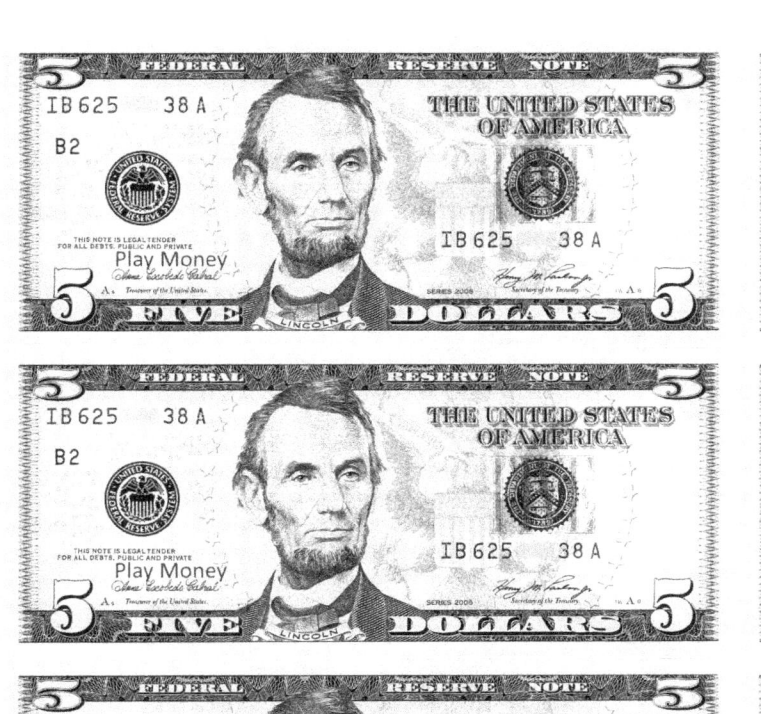

Learning With Money Activity Kit by David E. McAdams

Learning With Money Activity Kit by David E. McAdams

Learning With Money Activity Kit by David E. McAdams

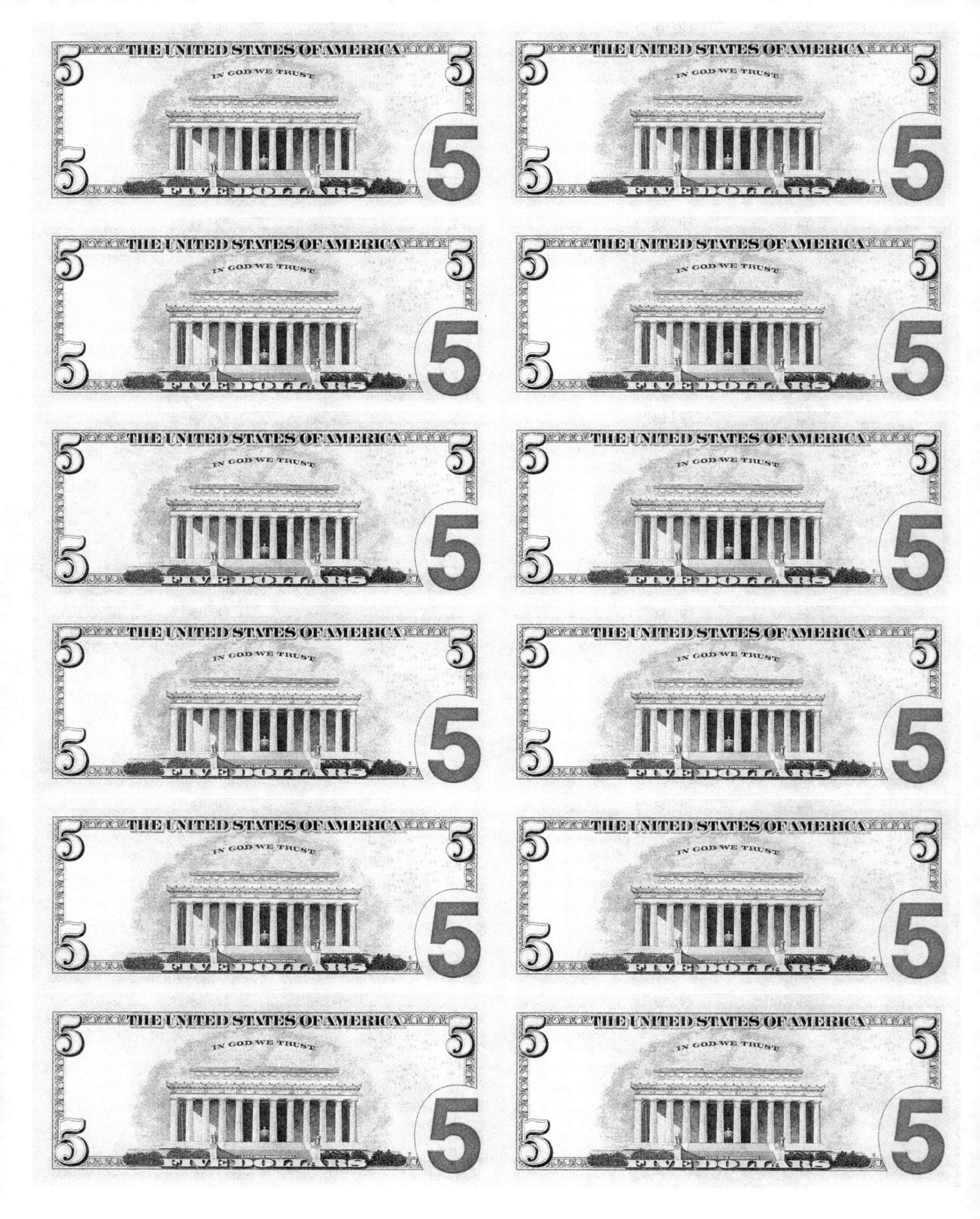

Learning With Money Activity Kit by David E. McAdams

Learning With Money Activity Kit by David E. McAdams

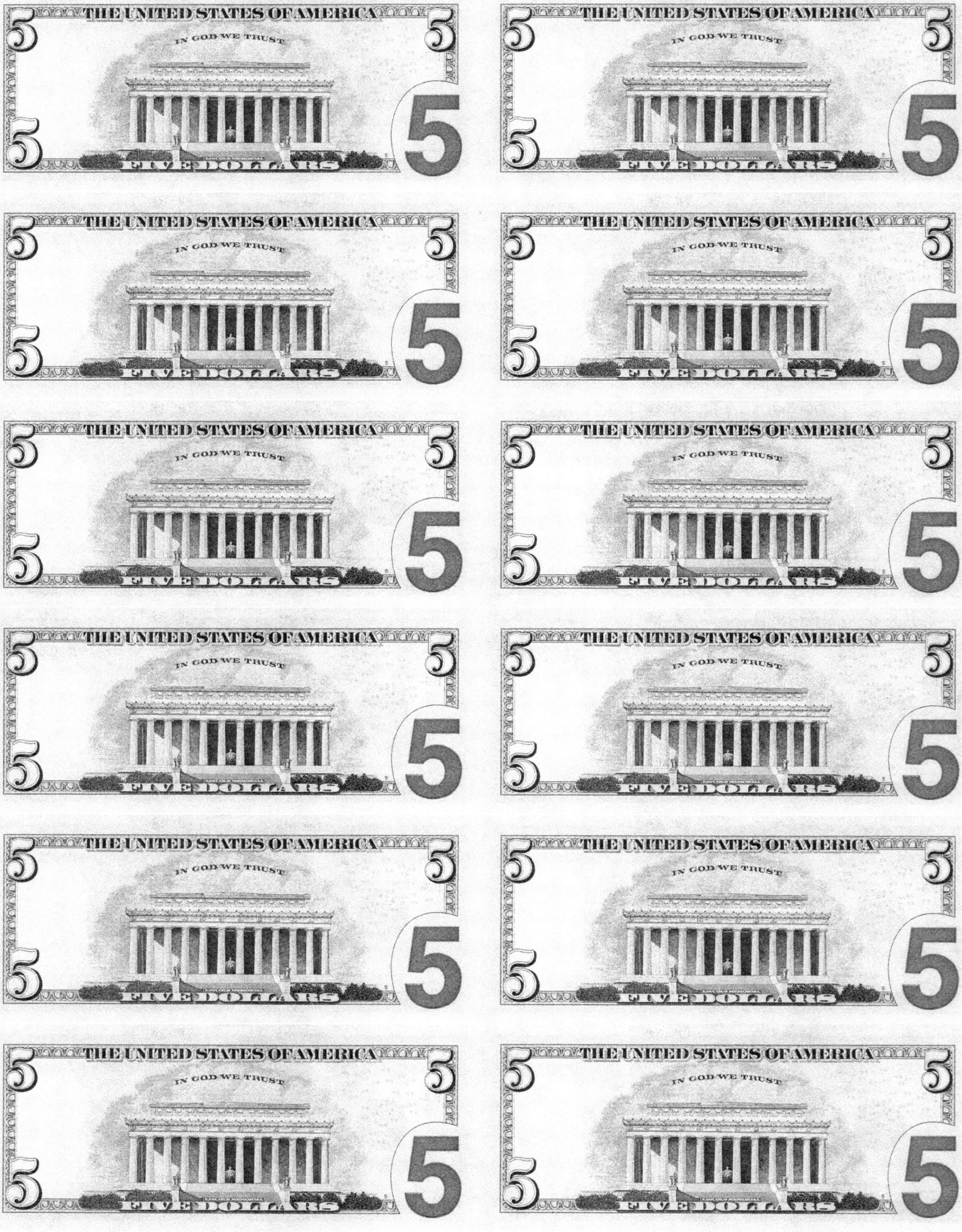
THE UNITED STATES OF AMERICA
IN GOD WE TRUST
FIVE DOLLARS
5

Learning With Money Activity Kit by David E. McAdams

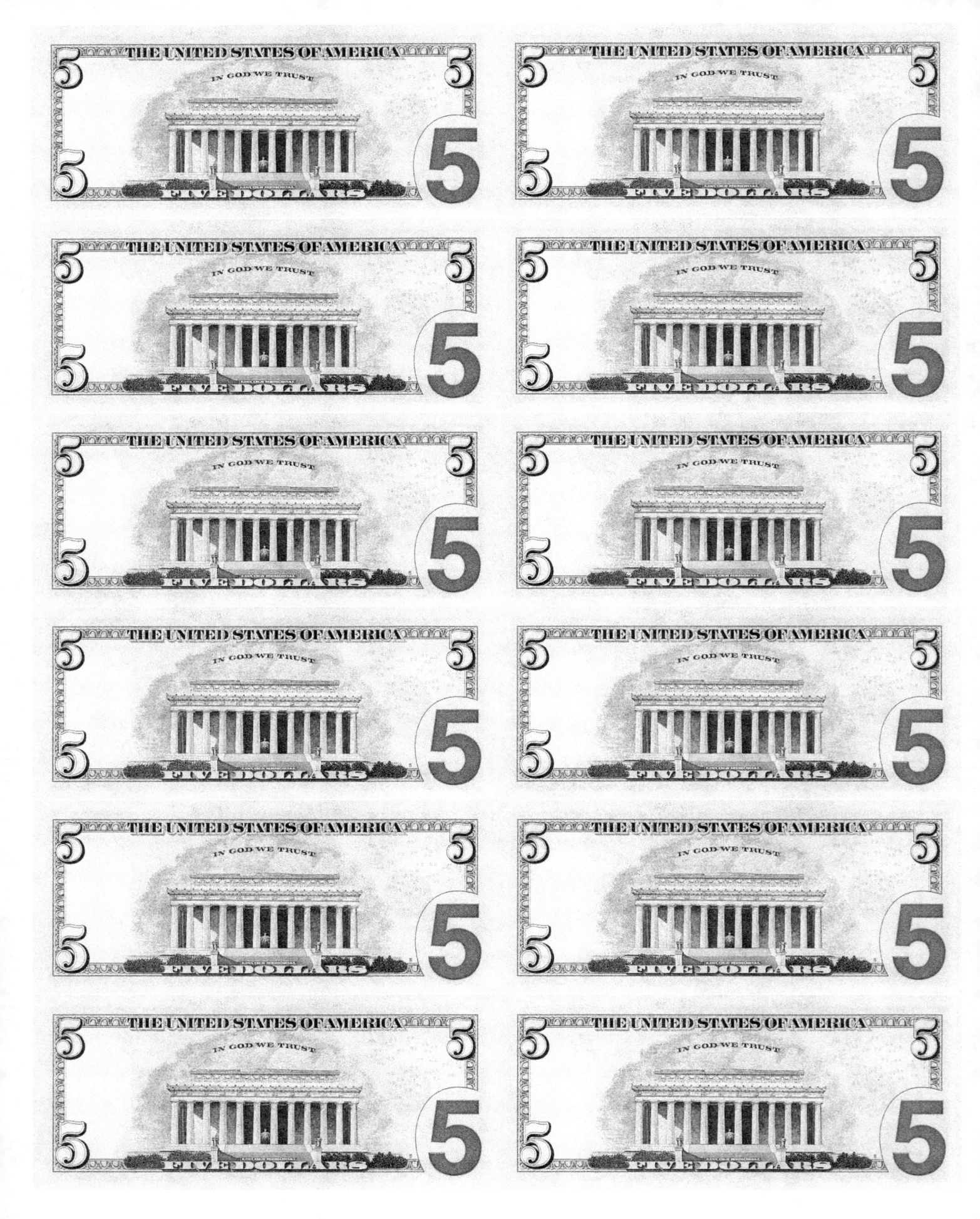

Learning With Money Activity Kit by David E. McAdams

Learning With Money Activity Kit by David E. McAdams 73

74   Learning With Money Activity Kit by David E. McAdams

Learning With Money Activity Kit by David E. McAdams

Learning With Money Activity Kit by David E. McAdams

Learning With Money Activity Kit by David E. McAdams

Learning With Money Activity Kit by David E. McAdams

Learning With Money Activity Kit by David E. McAdams

Learning With Money Activity Kit by David E. McAdams

Learning With Money Activity Kit by David E. McAdams

THE UNITED STATES OF AMERICA
IN GOD WE TRUST
ONE
ONE DOLLAR

THE UNITED STATES OF AMERICA
IN GOD WE TRUST
ONE
ONE DOLLAR

THE UNITED STATES OF AMERICA
IN GOD WE TRUST
ONE
ONE DOLLAR

THE UNITED STATES OF AMERICA
IN GOD WE TRUST
ONE
ONE DOLLAR

THE UNITED STATES OF AMERICA
IN GOD WE TRUST
ONE
ONE DOLLAR

THE UNITED STATES OF AMERICA
IN GOD WE TRUST
ONE
ONE DOLLAR

THE UNITED STATES OF AMERICA
IN GOD WE TRUST
ONE
ONE DOLLAR

THE UNITED STATES OF AMERICA
IN GOD WE TRUST
ONE
ONE DOLLAR

THE UNITED STATES OF AMERICA
IN GOD WE TRUST
ONE
ONE DOLLAR

THE UNITED STATES OF AMERICA
IN GOD WE TRUST
ONE
ONE DOLLAR

THE UNITED STATES OF AMERICA
IN GOD WE TRUST
ONE
ONE DOLLAR

THE UNITED STATES OF AMERICA
IN GOD WE TRUST
ONE
ONE DOLLAR

Learning With Money Activity Kit by David E. McAdams

Learning With Money Activity Kit by David E. McAdams

Learning With Money Activity Kit by David E. McAdams

Learning With Money Activity Kit by David E. McAdams

Learning With Money Activity Kit by David E. McAdams

Learning With Money Activity Kit by David E. McAdams

Learning With Money Activity Kit by David E. McAdams

Learning With Money Activity Kit by David E. McAdams

Learning With Money Activity Kit by David E. McAdams

Learning With Money Activity Kit by David E. McAdams

Learning With Money Activity Kit by David E. McAdams

Learning With Money Activity Kit by David E. McAdams

Learning With Money Activity Kit by David E. McAdams

Learning With Money Activity Kit by David E. McAdams

Learning With Money Activity Kit by David E. McAdams

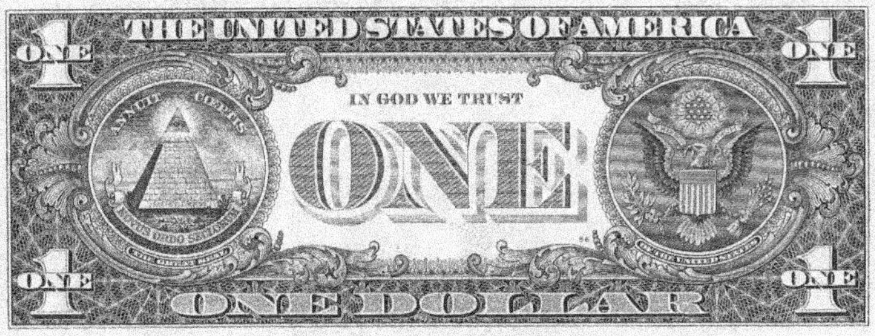

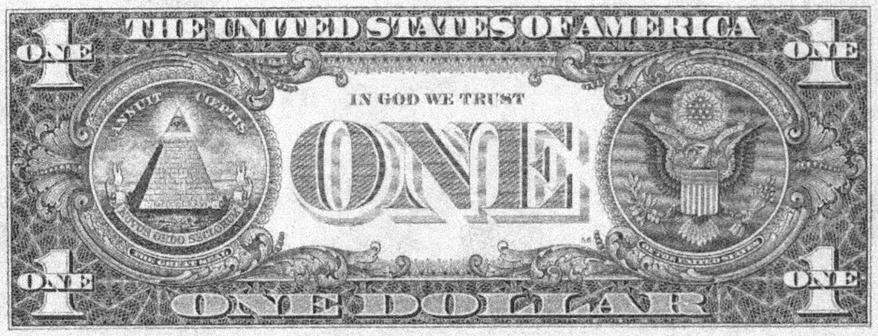

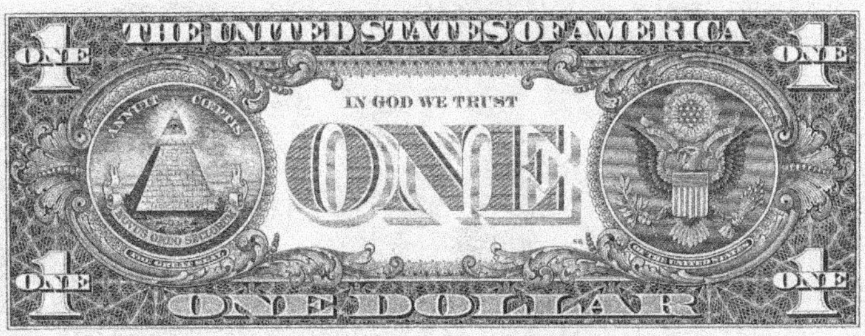

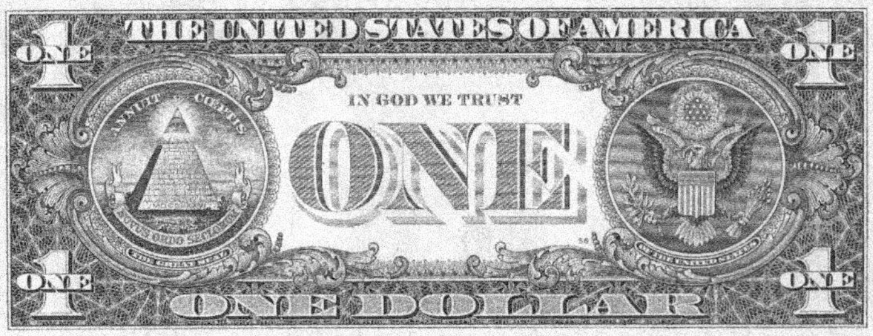

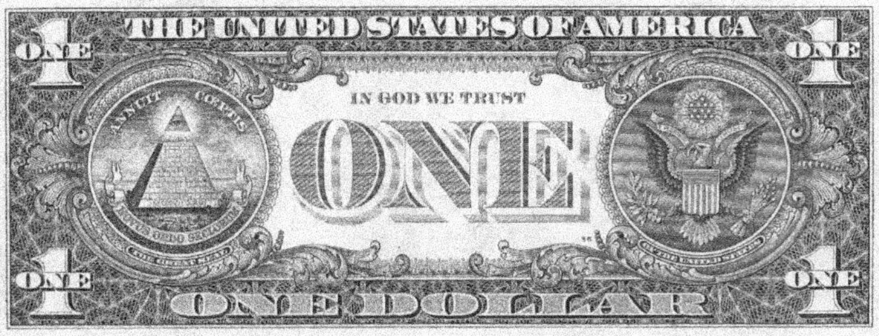

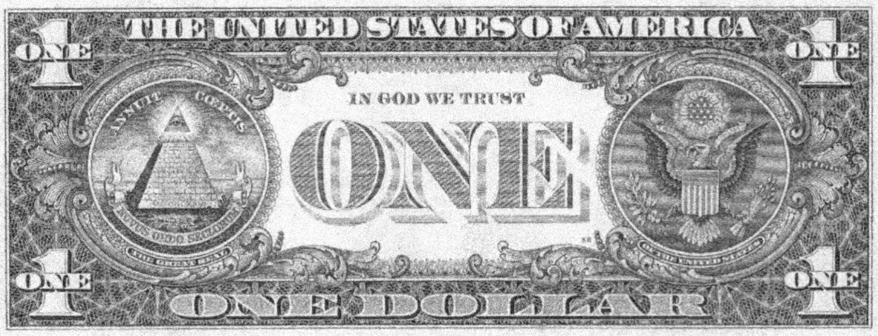

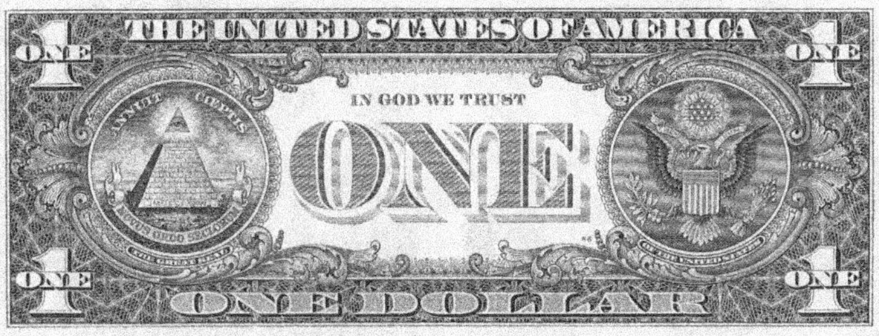

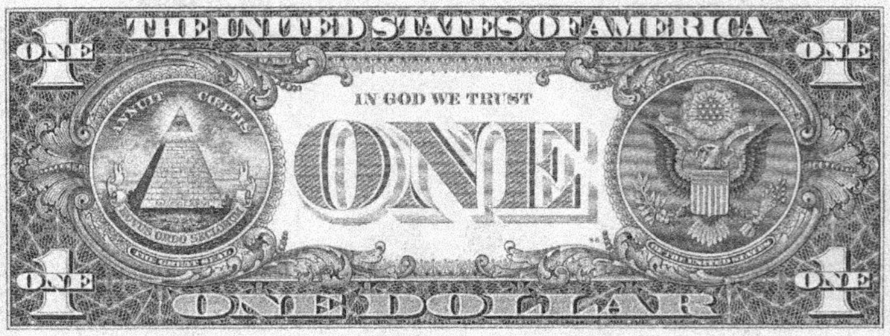

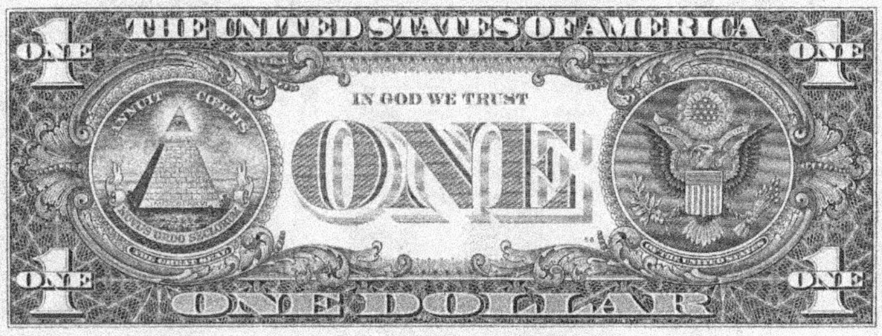

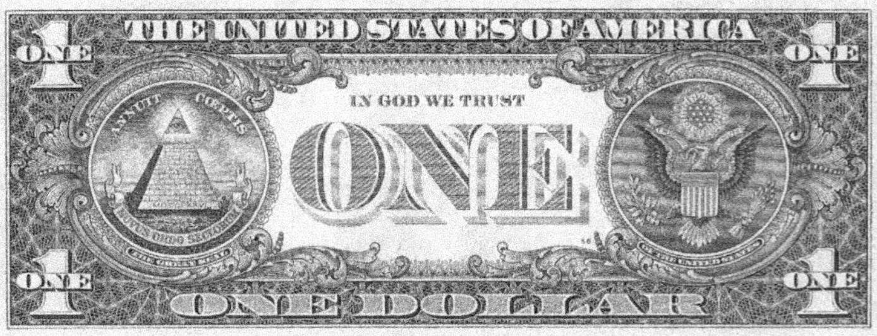

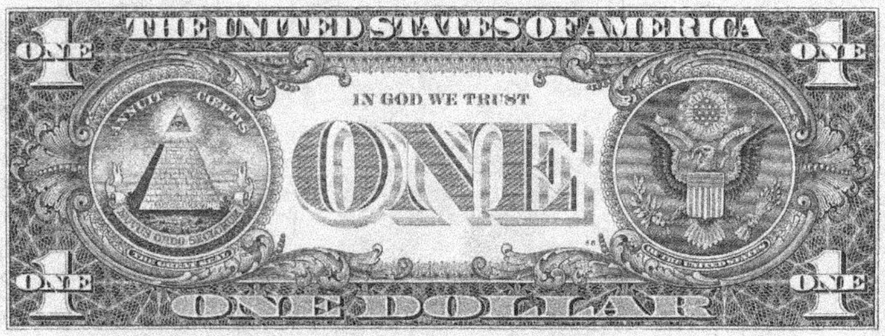

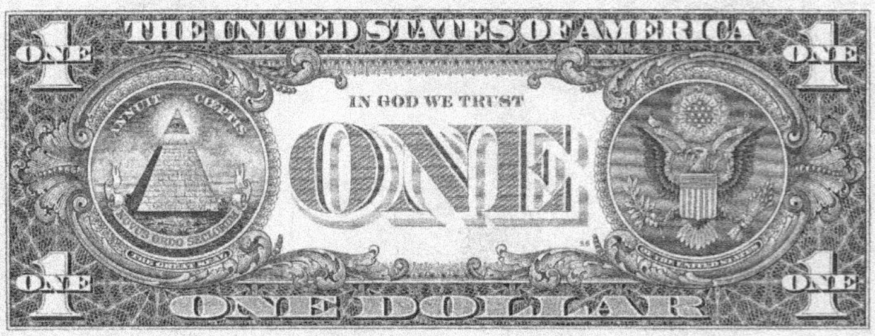

CPSIA information can be obtained
at www.ICGtesting.com
Printed in the USA
BVHW021201230623
666260BV00012B/699